CONTEMPORARY'S

WRITER'S MANUAL ACTIVITY BOOK 2

D1385321

EDWARD FRY, PH.D.

CONTENTS

Exercise 1: Writing Clearly 3

Exercise 2: Alphabetizing and Finding Words 4

Exercise 3: Vocabulary: Working with Homophones 5

Exercise 4: Spelling: Plurals, Suffixes, and Endings 6

Exercise 5: Spelling: Prefixes, *ei-ie*, and Compounds 7

Exercise 6: Phonics: Checking Correct Spelling 8

Exercise 7: Capitalization: Proper Nouns 9

Exercise 8: Capitalization: First Words and Titles. 10

Exercise 9: Punctuation: End Marks and Commas 11

Exercise 10: Punctuation: Writing Quotations 12

Exercise 11: Punctuation: The Apostrophe 13

Exercise 12: Grammar: Subjects and Predicates 14

Exercise 13: Grammar: Verbs and Agreement 15

Exercise 14: Grammar: Forming Verb Tenses 16

Exercise 15: Grammar: Using Modifiers in Sentences 17

Exercise 16: Grammar: Combining Sentences 18

Exercise 17: Writing Process 1: Prewriting 19

Exercise 18: Writing Process 2: Drafting 20

Exercise 19: Writing Process 3: Revising 21

Exercise 20: Writing Process 4: Proofreading 22

Exercise 21: Writing a Friendly Letter. 23

Exercise 22: Writing an Original Story 24

Exercise 23: Writing Instructions 25

Exercise 24: Writing a Description 26

Exercise 25: Writing To Persuade 27

Exercise 26: Literary Terms and Devices. 28

Answer Key 29

ISBN: 0-8092-0893-8

Published by Contemporary Books,
a division of NTC/Contemporary Publishing Group, Inc.,
4255 West Touhy Avenue,
Lincolnwood (Chicago), Illinois 60646-1975 U.S.A.
© 1997 by Edward Fry

EXERCISE 1   Writing Clearly

When you write, you have a message to share. It's important to your audience that your message is easy to understand. Reference works such as the *Writer's Manual* help you find the right words and right form for your work.

A. DIRECTIONS:

Review the table of contents on pages 3 and 4 of the *Writer's Manual*. Turn to each section of the book and make yourself familiar with the topics covered on those pages. Then answer these questions.

Example: What four topics are covered in Techniques for Composition?

Ways of Organizing Your Thoughts   *Story Starters*

Tips on Improving Your Vocabulary   *Literary Terms and Devices*

1. What are the six topics discussed in Mechanics of Writing? On what page does each topic begin?

   _____ p. ____   _____ p. ____

   _____ p. ____   _____ p. ____

   _____ p. ____   _____ p. ____

2. In Guidelines for Composition, there is a discussion of the Writing Process followed by sections on nine forms of writing. Which pages discuss the Writing Process? _____

3. List four of the forms of writing discussed in Guidelines for Composition.

   _____   _____

   _____   _____

B. DIRECTIONS:

Examine each error marked below. Decide which section of the *Writer's Manual* you would refer to in correcting the error. Write the name of that section after the number of the error. Error number 1 is done for you.

　　　¹　　　　　　　　²　　　　　　　　　　　　　　　　　　³　　　　　　⁴　　⁵
　　(during the 1920s,) several millionaires lived on Euclid (avenue). The beautyful (huje)

　　　　　　　　　　　　　　　　　⁶
homes stood on huge lots with colorful (guardens). Today most of these homes (is) gone.

Example: (1) _____ *Capitalization* _____

2. _____   5. _____

3. _____   6. _____

4. _____   7. _____

EXERCISE 2   Alphabetizing and Finding Words

The words in the Spelling Checker (pages 9–66) of the *Writer's Manual* are arranged in alphabetical order. Sets of guide letters on each page show the first two letters of every word listed on that page.

A. DIRECTIONS:

Rewrite each list of words below in alphabetical order.

Example: car   *apple*
         apple   *car*
         dog   *dog*

1. play   _____
   bright   _____
   rent   _____
   whale   _____

4. line   _____
   liberal   _____
   little   _____
   listen   _____

2. lever   _____
   exist   _____
   profit   _____
   handle   _____

5. exhaust   _____
   example   _____
   expand   _____
   excite   _____

3. fifty   _____
   family   _____
   flute   _____
   factory   _____

6. believe   _____
   belong   _____
   bell   _____
   belt   _____

B. DIRECTIONS:

In the Spelling Checker (pages 9–66) of the *Writer's Manual,* find each of the words listed under *Word* below. On the first line, write the two-letter guide under which you found the word. On the next line, write the page on which you found the word.

Example: geometry   *ge*   *28*

Word	2-Letter Guide	Page
1. liberate	____	____
2. commerce	____	____
3. organize	____	____
4. battery	____	____
5. success	____	____

EXERCISE 3   Vocabulary: Working with Homophones

Homophones are words that sound the same but are spelled differently and have different meanings.

You'll find seeds in the <u>core</u> of the apple.

This <u>corps</u> of soldiers is responsible for maintaining trucks.

The Spelling Checker on pages 9 through 66 of the *Writer's Manual* lists any homophones of a word under that word. The differences in meanings are also given.

A. DIRECTIONS:

To decide which word in parentheses belongs in each sentence below, find both words in the Spelling Checker. Compare their meanings. Then write the correct word on the line.

Example: (*disburse, disperse*) The British officer told the rebels to _____*disperse*_____.

1. (*cymbal, symbol*) In this poem, the snow is a _____ of innocence.

2. (*desert, dessert*) Do you want ice cream or sherbet for _____?

3. (*flair, flare*) In the talent show, Lisa displayed a real _____ for comedy.

4. (*gait, gate*) Till his ankle heals, Manuel will have an uneven _____.

5. (*dual, duel*) This car has a _____ brake system.

6. (*faint, feint*) The boxer's foe recognized his _____ and didn't fall back.

7. (*hoarse, horse*) I'm too _____ to sing today.

8. (*lessen, lesson*) Building a dike will _____ the chances of flooding.

B. DIRECTIONS:

There are three homophones in each set below. Refer to the Spelling Checker to find their meanings. Write the correct word in the sentence. Then choose one of the two remaining homophones and write a sentence that uses that homophone correctly.

Example: (*for, fore, four*) The fast walkers moved to the _____*fore*_____ of the hiking party.
_____*The group is known for singing folk songs.*_____

1. (*I, aye, eye*) All those who vote _____ on the issue should raise their hand.

   _____

2. (*you, ewe, yew*) Have _____ ever tried to train your dog?

   _____

3. (*burro, borough, burrow*) Which _____ of the city is the largest?

   _____

4. (*do, dew, due*) These library books are _____ on Friday.

   _____

Exercise 4   Spelling: Plurals, Suffixes, and Endings

The endings of many words change to show differences in meaning. For example, the noun *robot* changes to *robots* to indicate more than one robot. The verb *stop* in the sentence "Both cars stop" changes to *stops* in "Now one car stops," and to *stopped* in "Yesterday two cars stopped." In the *Writer's Manual*, the section on spelling rules (pages 67–68) provides guidelines on forming plurals and adding endings and suffixes to words.

A. DIRECTIONS:

Refer to the Spelling Rules section of the *Writer's Manual* (pages 67–68) to decide which word form in each item is correct. Underline the correct form.

Example: boxs, <u>boxes</u>

1. foods, foodes	4. playing, plaieing	7. (cross the) t's, ts	10. mouses, mice
2. bodys, bodies	5. videos, videoes	8. pupes, pups	11. noblely, nobly
3. brushs, brushes	6. sheeps, sheep	9. makeing, making	12. baited, baitted

B. DIRECTIONS:

Change each word in parentheses as indicated. Write the changed word. Then indicate which rule under Adding Endings and Suffixes (*Writer's Manual* pages 67–68) you followed.

Example: merry + ly   _____*merrily*_____   __e__

1. pretty + er   _____   _____

2. fine + er   _____   _____

3. admit + ed   _____   _____

4. pay + ment   _____   _____

5. garden + er   _____   _____

6. notable + ly   _____   _____

7. commit + ment   _____   _____

8. care + ful   _____   _____

C. DIRECTIONS:

Choose four of the words you formed in Activity B, above. Write a sentence using each word. Underline the word.

1. _____

2. _____

3. _____

4. _____

Answers begin on page 29.

EXERCISE 5 Spelling: Prefixes, *ei-ie*, and Compounds

These two spelling rules are true for many words:

(1) When you add a prefix to a word, or combine two words to make a compound word, no spelling or punctuation changes are needed.

(2) In words with *ei* or *ie*, write *i* before *e*, except after *c*.

Page 68 of the *Writer's Manual* discusses the exceptions to the rules.

A. DIRECTIONS:

Page 68 of the *Writer's Manual* will help you find the misspelled word in each sentence. Underline the word. Write it correctly on the line.

Example: That blockbuster movie went <u>unoticed</u> at first.   *unnoticed*

1. Our nieghbors trained their dog to walk backwards.   _____
2. That liar makes a science out of decieving people.   _____
3. Either Neil sped or he made an ilegal turn.   _____
4. No-body likes to misuse precious leisure time on errands.   _____
5. You must be self-motivated to complete your house-work.   _____

B. DIRECTIONS:

The prefixes *un-* and *im-* mean *not* or *to do the opposite of.* The prefix *re-* means *to do again.* For each sentence, decide which of these prefixes must be added to the word in parentheses to form the missing word. Refer to page 68 of the *Writer's Manual* for guidance in writing the new word.

Example: Because the table was so heavy, it was almost ___*immovable*___ (movable).

1. I got bored with my room, so I _____ (arranged) the furniture.
2. For centuries, people thought flying was _____ (possible).
3. The wall is newly painted and _____ (touched) by dirty hands.
4. The ball bearings are worn and must be _____ (placed).
5. Many citizens joined protests against the _____ (just) law.

C. DIRECTIONS:

Combine words from the box below to create at least four compound words. On a separate sheet of paper, write four sentences, each using a compound word you made. Underline the compound word in each sentence.

black	side	out	walk	board

Example: ___*blackboard*___ The teacher wrote on the <u>blackboard</u>.

1. _____   3. _____

2. _____   4. _____

Answers begin on page 29.

EXERCISE 6   Phonics: Checking Correct Spelling

In English, the same sound can be spelled in different ways. A word has only one correct spelling because each of its sounds is matched with only one of its possible spellings. Remember that although two homophones sound the same, you can't use the same spelling for both words. Each word has its own sound-spelling matchup.

DIRECTIONS:

In each item, look for a misspelled word or a homophone used incorrectly. Underline the misspelled or misused word. Write the correctly spelled word or the correct homophone on the line. If all of the words in the sentence are spelled correctly, write *Correct*.

Check the spelling of each suspicious word using the Spelling Checker of the *Writer's Manual* (pages 9–66). The charts in the Spelling Using Phonics section (pages 69–73) will direct you to different ways these sounds may be spelled.

Example: Was the package <u>dilivered</u> on time?   *delivered*

1. At noon, the bell told twelve times. _____
2. Gina drew the fence out of proportion to the house. _____
3. Lenny has been active in political campanes. _____
4. A bolder fell from the cliff and blocked the hiking trail. _____
5. You should take a photograph of this seen. _____
6. How could the owners let their house become so shabbie? _____
7. The settlers built a protective wall around their town. _____
8. Volunteers served delicious cookies at a party when the new liberry opened. _____
9. Now, the jury must decide whether this woman is innosent or guilty. _____
10. The organizers asked the City Counsel for a license to hold the parade. _____
11. Travelers can drive their automobiles onto the fairy. _____
12. The dogs are trained to recognize dangerous situations. _____
13. It's easy to locate the kemicals in this formula. _____
14. This map shows the locayshun of the buried treasure. _____
15. His explanation was too technical for me to understand. _____
16. A passenger on the cruise ship fell overbored. _____
17. The exercise room has two stationery bicycles. _____
18. A graff on page 206 tracks the growth of population in the city. _____
19. The worker left his hamer and nails on the floor. _____
20. Look up the defanition in the dictionary. _____

Answers begin on page 29.

EXERCISE 7   Capitalization: Proper Nouns

Proper nouns are words that name particular persons, places, and things. Begin each proper noun with a capital letter to set it apart from other words. See the Capitalization section on pages 74 to 75 in the *Writer's Manual* for more capitalization guidelines.

A. DIRECTIONS:

The sentences below have not been capitalized correctly. Rewrite each sentence on the line, using correct capitalization. If you need help, see pages 74 to 75 of the *Writer's Manual*.

Example: marian anderson sang in front of the lincoln memorial.
        Marian Anderson sang in front of the Lincoln Memorial.

1. brenda is head cashier at the bigger burger just east of town.

2. Last friday, the irish ambassador arrived in the united states.

3. Everyone knows that labor day marks the end of summer.

4. My ethnic background is a mixture of mexican, german, and french.

5. ivan plans to begin classes at the university of arizona next september.

6. I attend the united congregational church on delancey street.

B. DIRECTIONS:

For each category below, think of one proper noun. Then use it in a sentence. Be sure to capitalize correctly. If necessary, refer to pages 74 to 75 of the *Writer's Manual* to complete this activity.

Example: titles   *Sally interviewed **Doctor** Ibanes about his new book.*

1. schools

2. streets

3. trade names

4. countries

5. holidays

Exercise 8 Capitalization: First Words and Titles

Capitalize the first word in sentences, lines of most poetry, and quotations. Capitalize all the main words in titles of works such as poems, books, movies, and plays. Pages 74 and 75 of the *Writer's Manual* give you further guidelines for capitalization.

A. DIRECTIONS:

Underline the word or words that should be capitalized in each sentence or line of poetry. Remember that proper nouns should be capitalized, too. If you need help, refer to the section on capitalization in the *Writer's Manual* (pages 74–75).

Example: <u>my</u> uncle's family will visit us at <u>christmas</u>.

1. the flight attendant said, "fasten your seat belts, please."
2. *macavity, macavity, there's no one like macavity,*
   he's broken every human law, he breaks the law of gravity.
   his powers of levitation would make a fakir stare,
   and when you reach the scene of crime—macavity's not there!
      —T. S. Eliot, "Macavity: The Mystery Cat"
3. the menu included photos of the restaurant's best dishes.
4. tell me more about these "special circumstances."
5. our class read the classic book by stephen crane called *the red badge of courage.*
6. *water, water, everywhere,*
   and all the boards did shrink;
   water, water, everywhere,
   nor any drop to drink.
      —Samuel Taylor Coleridge, "The Rime of the Ancient Mariner"

B. DIRECTIONS:

Think of an existing title for each category. Write it on the line and capitalize it correctly. If you need help, refer to the capitalization rules on pages 74 and 75 of the *Writer's Manual.*

Example: book   *A Tale of Two Cities*
_____

1. book   _____

2. song   _____

3. TV program _____

Answers begin on page 29.

EXERCISE 9   Punctuation: End Marks and Commas

End marks after sentences tell readers whether the sentences are statements, orders, questions, or exclamations. Commas are important punctuation marks that are used for a variety of reasons. Read more about end marks and commas in the Punctuation section (pages 76 and 77) of the *Writer's Manual*.

A. DIRECTIONS:

Look at the end mark used in each sentence. If the end mark is correct, write *Correct* on the line. If a different end mark is needed, cross out the one that is there and write the correct end mark on the line. The Punctuation section (pages 76 and 77) of the *Writer's Manual* may help you.

Example: This song always reminds me of summer nights? ___.___

1. Do you recognize the lead actors in this movie? _____
2. How incredibly complex the human body is. _____
3. The train is always crowded at rush hour? _____
4. You'll find the new schedule posted on the bulletin board. _____
5. Will you be able to attend the graduation ceremony! _____
6. Stack these books in a pile on the floor, please. _____

B. DIRECTIONS:

Insert commas where they are needed in the friendly letter below. Refer to page 77 of the *Writer's Manual* for more information about using commas.

Example: Matt plays soccer, baseball, and basketball.

Dear Marisa
    How are you? I can't believe that I haven't seen you since your birthday on April 25 1995. So much has happened since then. Cheryl my best friend has moved to Albany New York. After she left I felt lonely for a while. But I have taken up some hobbies. Now I run swim and play tennis. Some friends recently asked "Why not play handball?" I guess that will be my next sport.
    I have also done some traveling. I discovered that I like the warm friendly slow-paced atmosphere of the South. I just heard about a sports convention that will be held in Atlanta Georgia and I am planning to attend. I read that over 10000 people attended the organization's last convention.
    I hope to see you soon. Maybe I can stop by on my way to Atlanta on September 6 1997.

                              Your cousin
                              Leslie

EXERCISE 10   Punctuation: Writing Quotations

A direct quotation repeats a person's exact words. Use quotation marks and a comma to set off a direct quotation from the rest of the sentence. The Punctuation section (pages 76–77) in the *Writer's Manual* explains more about using quotation marks and commas.

A. DIRECTIONS:

Insert quotation marks and commas where they are needed in the following sentences. If you need help, refer to pages 76–77 of the *Writer's Manual*.

Example: "Look up that word in the dictionary," suggested Pat.

1. I'm sure you would enjoy a visit to Australia said the travel agent.
2. Lee asked Which instrument do you play in the orchestra?
3. I can't figure out how to program this answering machine complained Dardreana.
4. The eye doctor asked Can you read the first line of letters on the chart?
5. The marchers will start at Public Square and go all the way to the lakefront explained the news announcer.
6. Steve shouted I got tickets to the play-off game!
7. Be careful when you pick up that glass figurine warned Marquita.
8. The worried astronaut said Houston, we have a problem.
9. I believe that my experience qualifies me for this job asserted James.
10. The loss of our rain forests is a global problem reported the scientist.

B. DIRECTIONS:

Complete the following sentences with a direct quotation. Refer to *Writer's Manual* pages 76–77 for help with punctuating direct quotations.

Example: The experienced hiker warned , *"Be sure to carry plenty of water."*

1. As it looked at Earth for the first time, the Martian visitor said

   _____

2. When he knew that he had won the election, the new president shouted

   _____

3. _____ whispered the librarian.

4. _____ suggested the loan officer.

Answers begin on page 29.

EXERCISE 11   Punctuation: The Apostrophe

The apostrophe has several uses. First, apostrophes show possession. For example, in the phrase *Burt's home*, the apostrophe shows that the home belongs to Burt. Apostrophes also show that letters or numbers have been omitted. For example, in the contraction *wasn't*, the apostrophe shows that the letters *no* (was <u>not</u>) have been omitted. Refer to the Punctuation section (page 76) and the Apostrophe section (pages 78–79) in the *Writer's Manual* for further discussion about using the apostrophe.

A. DIRECTIONS

Rewrite the underlined word in each sentence to show possession. Refer to the Apostrophe section (pages 78–79) in the *Writer's Manual* for help in completing this activity.

Example: A healthy <u>dog</u> coat is usually soft and shiny. _____*dog's*_____

1. The <u>farmer</u> tractor is unbelievably expensive. _____

2. The <u>skaters</u> outfits were covered with rhinestones and lace. _____

3. The <u>chairman</u> voice carried easily over the noise of the convention. _____

4. The science world applauded <u>Watson and Crick</u> discoveries. _____

5. We hope that it will be possible to restore my <u>grandmother</u> quilts. _____

6. <u>Dr. Simmons</u> office is both modern and comfortable. _____

7. That must be <u>someone else</u> responsibility, not mine. _____

8. The Johnsons have borrowed the <u>Muellers</u> camper van. _____

9. <u>Carmen and Gina</u> family is moving to Elmwood Street. _____

10. All of the writers were anxious to hear the <u>editor-in-chief</u> opinion. _____

B. DIRECTIONS:

For each word group below, write a contraction that has the same meaning. Be sure to use the apostrophe correctly. Refer to the Apostrophe (pages 78–79) and Contractions (page 83) sections in the *Writer's Manual* for help in completing this activity.

Example: should not _____*shouldn't*_____

1. could not _____
2. she will _____
3. we would _____
4. I am _____
5. will not _____

6. I have _____
7. cannot _____
8. he is _____
9. we are _____
10. what is _____

Answers begin on page 30.

EXERCISE 12   Grammar: Subjects and Predicates

Every complete sentence has two parts, the subject and the predicate. You will find an explanation of both of these sentence parts in the Grammar section of the *Writer's Manual* (pages 84–94).

A. DIRECTIONS:

Provide a complete subject for each of these predicates. Provide subjects that are longer than one word. For more information on complete subjects, see pages 84 to 85 of the *Writer's Manual*.

Example: <u>Students in the home ec class</u> prepared a fine meal.

1. _____ bought lottery tickets at the gas station.
2. _____ has a habit of being slow.
3. _____ may return late at night.
4. _____ flew north over the lake.

B. DIRECTIONS:

Provide a complete predicate for each of these subjects. Provide predicates that are longer than one word. For more information on complete predicates, see pages 84 to 85 of the *Writer's Manual*.

Example: The plant with drooping leaves _____*needs water*_____.

1. Every salesperson in the store _____.
2. The twins _____.
3. My two closest friends _____.
4. Many flowers in the garden _____.

C. DIRECTIONS:

Decide whether each of these items is a subject, predicate, or complete sentence. If it is none of these, call it a phrase. On the line, write *subject, predicate, sentence,* or *phrase*.

Example: At the theater in the mall _____*phrase*_____

1. A bandit stopped the stagecoach _____
2. The steady sound of raindrops _____
3. Across the floor with loose boards _____
4. Falls asleep during the TV news shows _____
5. Scored the winning touchdown _____

Exercise 13   Grammar: Verbs and Agreement

Verbs must agree with their subjects in both person and number. For further explanation of this topic, see pages 89 to 90 in the *Writer's Manual*, Verb Errors, Error Number 1.

A. DIRECTIONS:

Underline the correct verb form to complete each sentence.

Example: Grandpa *(remember, remembers)* when this street wasn't paved.

1. Nancy *(know, knows)* all the words to the French national anthem.

2. To get to my house, you *(exit, exits)* the freeway at Grant Avenue.

3. We always *(enjoy, enjoys)* the summer band concerts in the park.

4. The author *(cite, cites)* several leading authorities in her new book.

5. Flowers *(bloom, blooms)* nonstop in my yard from spring to fall.

6. Each year, the judges *(select, selects)* the winner of the contest.

B. DIRECTIONS:

Complete each sentence with a present-tense form of the irregular verb *be*. Make sure the verb agrees with the subject in both number and person. To complete this activity, refer to the chart on page 90 in the *Writer's Manual*.

Example: Ed _____*is*_____ an expert chess player.

1. You _____ the most persistent person I have ever known!

2. Many animals _____ not able to distinguish between colors.

3. Computer programming _____ a useful skill to have for job hunting.

4. I _____ not familiar with that variety of tomato.

5. We _____ eager to see the new movie based on the popular novel.

6. You _____ welcome to join us at the theater, if you'd like.

C. DIRECTIONS:

Choose one of the verb forms listed below. Circle it. Then write a sentence in which the verb agrees with its subject in number and person.

make	**ride**	**see**
makes	**rides**	**sees**

EXERCISE 14   Grammar: Forming Verb Tenses

When a verb changes its form to show *when* an action happens, we say it changes its tense. The three major tenses correspond to the three times when actions can take place—the future, the present, and the past. To learn more about verb tenses, read pages 90 to 92 in the *Writer's Manual*.

A. DIRECTIONS:

Underline the correct verb form in each of the following sentences. If you need help, refer to the Verb Errors section, Error Numbers 2 and 3, on pages 90 to 91 in the *Writer's Manual*.

Example: Mark *(will know, knew)* all the answers on yesterday's TV game show.

1. The squirrels *(are digging, digging)* up all my tulip bulbs!

2. Tomorrow, I *(took, will take)* a qualifying test for a new job.

3. The waiter *(has filled, have filled)* all of the salt and pepper shakers.

4. We *(have been, will be)* at the airport when your flight arrives tonight.

5. You *(blocking, are blocking)* my view of the television screen.

6. When I say the magic words, a rabbit *(popped, will pop)* out of my hat.

7. Some students *(have formed, has formed)* a committee to study the problem.

8. Rocky *(will play, played)* second base for ten years before he retired.

9. The mountain climbers *(tackling, will tackle)* the highest peak tomorrow.

10. We *(has waited, have waited)* in line for this ride for over an hour.

11. After several days without rain, the flowers *(wilting, wilted)* and died.

12. My neighbor *(have been, has been)* a member of the school board for years.

B. DIRECTIONS:

Complete each sentence with a helping verb and the past participle of the verb in parentheses. The helping verb should be either *has* or *have*. If necessary, refer to the Verb Errors section, Error Number 5 (page 91) and the irregular verbs chart (page 92) in the *Writer's Manual*.

Example: The candidate *(throw)* _has thrown_ her hat into the ring.

1. The gold medal winner *(swim)* _____ since she was three.

2. Teresa *(catch)* _____ the virus that has been going around.

3. The new citizens *(take)* _____ an oath of allegiance to their new country.

4. I *(wear)* _____ my grandfather's gold watch ever since he died.

5. You *(be)* _____ an honest and trustworthy friend.

   Answers begin on page 30.

EXERCISE 15 Grammar: Using Modifiers in Sentences

A basic sentence needs just a noun for the subject and a verb for the predicate. However, sentences usually include other parts of speech. Adjectives, adverbs, and other words give detail and interest to sentences. The Grammar section of the *Writer's Manual* explains the parts of speech on pages 93 to 94.

DIRECTIONS:

Read each of these sentences and mark them to answer the questions below. The *Writer's Manual* sections Sentences: Basic Construction (pages 84–86) and Parts of Speech (pages 93–94) will help you.

Example: A weather front <u>in the west</u> will bring us snow.
   Direction: Underline the prepositional phrase.

(1) Gene said that his meal at the Corner Cafe last night was a disaster. (2) The salad was remarkably tasteless. (3) In the main course, a lump of cold mashed potatoes sat at the side of a dry slice of ham. (4) The chef there obviously had little interest in cooking. (5) Gene complained rather loudly to the unlucky waitress. (6) Customers won't return.

1. In sentence 1, underline the prepositional phrase. Which noun does it modify?

   _____

2. Circle the adjective in sentence 2. Which noun does it modify? _____

3. Underline the adverb in sentence 2. Does it modify a verb, an adjective, or another adverb?

   _____

4. Five prepositional phrases appear in sentence 3, but they use only three different prepositions. Write those three prepositions. _____

5. Underline the prepositional phrase that modifies *lump*. Circle the adjective(s) in that prepositional phrase. Box the noun modified by the adjective(s).

6. (a) In sentences 4 and 5, underline every adverb.

   (b) Write *H* above each adverb that answers the question *How?* Write *W* above each adverb that answers the question *Where?* Write *T* above each adverb that answers *To what degree?* (or *How much?*).

   (c) In which sentence, 4 or 5, does an adverb modify another adverb? _____

7. Rewrite sentence 6. Add these modifiers: (a) an adjective modifying *Customers*; (b) a prepositional phrase that modifies *won't return* and answers the question *Where?*; (c) an adverb that modifies *won't return* and answers the question *When?*

EXERCISE 16   Grammar: Combining Sentences

Pronouns stand for nouns. Some examples of pronouns are *you, we, that, it, who, whom,* and *which.*
Conjunctions, such as *and* and *although,* join individual words or groups of words. Both types of words are useful in combining sentences, as in these examples.

Luis has our club's old exercise bike. Luis never uses the bike.

(1) Luis has our club's old exercise bike, **which** he never uses.

(2) **Although** Luis has our club's old exercise bike, he never uses **it.**

The *Writer's Manual* provides more information about the parts of speech and about combining sentences on pages 84 to 86 and 93 to 94.

A. DIRECTIONS:

For each item, combine the given sentences using the listed conjunction and/or pronoun in place of a repeated phrase. Refer to the *Writer's Manual* as needed.

Example: I saw the banner. The banner was already torn.

(*when, it*) *The banner was already torn when I saw it.*

1. The mountain climbers set out. Snow was beginning to fall.

    (*although*) _____

2. During the storm, a tree fell on a car. The car belonged to Darlene Stewart.

    (*that*) _____

3. Keith waved to Rosa at the mall yesterday. Rosa didn't notice Keith.

    (*but, she, him*) _____

4. You are looking for a talented dancer. I am the talented dancer.

    (*whom*) _____

5. We threw out the old blue vase. The old blue vase was leaking.

    (*which*) _____

6. The storm may stay out at sea. The storm may clobber the coast.

    (*or, it*) _____

B. DIRECTIONS:

This sentence combines several sentences incorrectly. Rewrite it as one or more correct sentences.

Baby Janice loves to listen to stories and some sitters know many stories and they tell them well and Janice always behaves for those sitters.

_____

_____

EXERCISE 17   Writing Process 1: Prewriting

Most people find that they produce their best writing when they work through five steps. Together, these steps are called the *writing process*. For more information on the writing process, see pages 97 through 103 of the *Writer's Manual*. The first step in the writing process involves getting and organizing ideas.

A. DIRECTIONS:

Read about the prewriting stage on pages 97 and 98 of the *Writer's Manual*. Then choose one of the situations listed below, and circle its number. Use brainstorming to come up with at least five topics you could write about in that situation. List them.

Situations:

1. Persuading people to vote for a candidate for office
2. Describing a building familiar to you
3. Explaining how a certain appliance works

Example: (2) the apartment building I live in, my church, the grocery store on Third Street, Mayfield Center Theater, the gas station where I work

B. DIRECTIONS:

Choose one of the topics listed in Activity A, either in the sample or your answer. Write that topic in the circle at the center of the graph below. Think of details that develop that topic and list them in the other four circles. Add more circles and details, if you like.

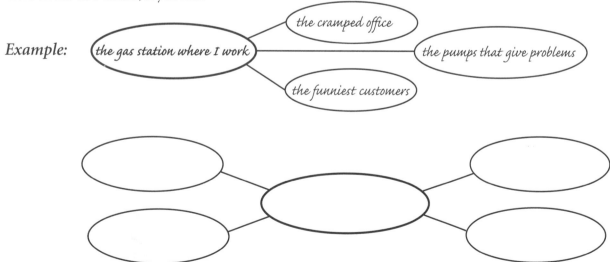

Example: the gas station where I work — the cramped office — the pumps that give problems — the funniest customers

EXERCISE 18   Writing Process 2: Drafting

During prewriting, a writer makes notes about what he or she will discuss. The writer often creates graphs or outlines to suggest the relationship of ideas. During the second stage of the writing process, called *drafting*, the writer turns these notes into sentences and paragraphs. Pages 98 through 99 of the *Writer's Manual* suggest some approaches to this task.

DIRECTIONS:

Read the following notes for an explanation of a process. The writer has numbered the notes in an order that seems reasonable. Draft the explanation. Begin your draft on the lines below. Try to begin with a topic sentence. Use extra paper as needed.

How a lock works

2   Boat floats on river or canal to lock

4   Lock gate closes behind boat

1   Water on different sides of lock is at different levels

3   Water in lock has to be at same level as the side the boat is on so that the boat can float in

5   When boat is inside, and gate behind it is shut, the gate at the far end of lock opens slowly

6   If water inside lock is higher than water beyond far gate, lock water spills out gradually until the water level inside matches water level beyond

    If water inside lock is lower than water beyond far gate, water from beyond gate spills gradually into lock; water level rises, lifting boat to higher level

7   When water inside lock is at same level as water beyond, far gate opens wide

Answers begin on page 30.

In the third stage of the writing process, a writer takes a careful look at the draft and makes changes to the content, that is, what it says. Pages 100 to 102 of the *Writer's Manual* provide guidelines for revising your writing in general and also give suggestions for revising specific types of writing.

DIRECTIONS:

Read the following draft, keeping in mind the guidelines on pages 100 to 102 of the *Writer's Manual*. Then answer the questions below.

> ~~A whole lot of~~ cities in Ohio are named after cities in other countries. ~~Looking at a map, you can see a~~ London, as in England; ~~a~~ Dublin, as in Ireland; and ~~a~~ Rome, as in Italy. On Ohio's map you can see the names *Milan,* as in Italy; *Berlin,* as in Germany; and *Lima,* as in Peru. But you can't tell from looking at the map that Ohio's *Milan* and *Berlin* are pronounced with the accent on the first syllable, unlike the European city names, ~~or~~ that Ohio's *Lima* has a long /i/ sound instead of the long /e/ sound in Peru's *Lima.* There are Athens, as in Greece; Antioch, as in Turkey; and Alexandria, as in Egypt. ~~By the way, Wisconsin has a Sparta to go with Ohio's Athens.~~

Many

In Ohio you'll find

(*Insert*)

Nor can you tell

1. Compare the original sentence 2 with the original sentence 3. How does the revision to sentence 2 improve the way the sentences fit together? _____

    _____

2. Why did the writer delete the last sentence of the original paragraph?

    _____

3. Why did the writer move the sentence that mentions Athens to become sentence 3?

    _____

    _____

4. Why did the writer put the information about Lima in a sentence of its own?

    _____

5. Which addition does the paragraph need more, a new opening sentence or an ending sentence? Give a reason for your answer. _____

    _____

EXERCISE 20 Writing Process 4: Proofreading

In the fourth stage of the writing process, a writer reviews the revised work and looks for mistakes in such details as spelling, punctuation, and grammar. Pages 102 to 103 of the *Writer's Manual* provide guidelines for proofreading, and page 104 shows how to mark corrections. When all corrections have been made, the writer makes a clean copy of his or her work. See page 103 of the *Writer's Manual* for ways to share your writing.

DIRECTIONS:

Proofread these sentences for errors in grammar, spelling, capitalization, and punctuation. Each sentence has at least two errors. Mark the errors using proofreading symbols as shown in the second column on page 104 of the *Writer's Manual*. Then write the sentence correctly on the following line.

Example: The officer shouted angrily, get those cannons over hear!

The officer shouted angrily, "Get those cannons over here!"

1. You wont need to see Dr campbell until 6 Months from now.

   _____

2. The latest versions of that computer Program, has several glitchs.

   _____

3. My neighbor up-stairs said "that she was going too retire soon."

   _____

4. Mailee steered the car i pushed it and jack just stood and watched.

   _____

5. "Its time for bed," Ms Kantor said. "Im not tired," junior objected.

   _____

6. How beautyful the Sky is tonight, full stars!

   _____

7. The Smith's went to africa on they're vacation.

   _____

8. Has the furniture in the bed room been payed for yet

   _____

Answers begin on page 30.

EXERCISE 21   Writing a Friendly Letter

A friendly letter is a good way to keep in touch with friends and relatives, especially when they live far away. A thank-you note uses the same format as a friendly letter. See page 106 in the *Writer's Manual* for an example of the usual form for a friendly letter.

A. DIRECTIONS:

Match each part of a friendly letter with an example of that part. Write the letter of the example beside the name of the part it matches. Refer to page 106 in the *Writer's Manual* if you need help.

Example: _____a_____ Greeting   a.   Dear Jim,

1. _____ Greeting   a.   Thank you for sharing your lake house with me last weekend. I had a great time. I hope you can visit me in the city next winter.

2. _____ Signature   b.   Yours truly,

3. _____ Closing   c.   Dear Ellen,

4. _____ Body   d.   *Gina*

5. _____ Heading   e.   14450 Tower St.
                                 Marlboro, MA 01752
                                 August 18, 1997

B. DIRECTIONS:

On the lines below, write a thank-you note from Dave to his Aunt Lucy. Use this information as you write: Dave is writing on October 31, 1997, to thank his aunt for a gift. He lives at 3579 Wood Road in Los Angeles, California. His ZIP code is 90048. Follow the format for a friendly letter and write your own message in the body of the note. See page 106 in the *Writer's Manual* if you need help.

EXERCISE 22   Writing an Original Story

Stories have three major elements—characters, a setting, and a plot. Some stories tell about a true, personal experience. Others are entirely imaginary, with fantastic characters and events. To learn more about the elements of stories, read pages 108 and 109 in the *Writer's Manual*.

A. DIRECTIONS:

Begin to plan an original story. Think about whether you prefer to describe a personal experience or write a fantasy. For each type of story, decide who would be your characters, where and when the story would take place, and what the problem would be. Write some possibilities on the lines below.

Example: **Personal Experience**   **Fantasy**

Characters: *my friend Alex and I*   *time travelers*
Setting: *on a city street in 1996*   *in a jungle in prehistoric times*
Conflict: *find a wallet filled with money*   *have to battle dinosaurs*

Personal Experience   **Fantasy**

Characters: _____   _____

Setting: _____   _____

Conflict: _____   _____

B. DIRECTIONS:

Choose one type of story—personal experience or fantasy—to write. Circle the list above of characters, setting, and conflict that you will use. Now, plan the plot of the story. Decide what happens first, second, and so on. Think about what will happen at the end. Briefly describe events in each part of the story in time order. Refer to page 108 in the *Writer's Manual* for an example.

Rising Action: _____

_____

_____

Climax: _____

Falling Action: _____

Resolution: _____

C. DIRECTIONS:

On a separate sheet of paper or on a computer, write your story. Be sure to give it a title. Begin with an introduction. Use the plans you recorded in Activity B and add details and descriptions to make your story more vivid. For more tips on story writing, see the *Writer's Manual* (page 108).

EXERCISE 23 Writing Instructions

Good instructions are clear and logical. All of the steps needed to complete a task are described. No important steps are left out, and no unnecessary details are included. Steps are arranged in the order in which they are to be performed. You can learn more about writing instructions by reading page 112 of the *Writer's Manual.*

A. DIRECTIONS:

The steps below for baking bread are listed in the wrong order. Read the steps and decide on the correct time order. Then write complete instructions for baking bread that include all the steps, plus a topic sentence and a conclusion. See page 112 of the *Writer's Manual* for more about writing instructions.

- Punch down the risen dough, roll it into a rectangle, roll it up, and put it in a pan.

- First, stir together all the ingredients, beating until the mixture is smooth.

- Take the smooth mixture and knead it on a floured board for about ten minutes.

- Last, bake the bread at 425 degrees for about 35 minutes.

- After you finish kneading the dough, place it in a greased bowl and wait about an hour for it to rise the first time.

- Let the dough rise again in the pan.

_____

_____

_____

_____

_____

_____

_____

_____

B. DIRECTIONS:

Think of a task you know well. As you think of the steps it takes to complete the task, write them down on the lines. Then reread your list and number the steps in order. Write complete instructions for the task on a separate sheet of paper or on a computer.

Task: _____

_____ _____

_____ _____

_____ _____

EXERCISE 24   Writing a Description

You write a description to share an experience with your readers. To make the experience as real as possible, include exact details that appeal to all the senses. See page 114 of the *Writer's Manual* for suggestions for organizing and presenting the details of a description.

A. DIRECTIONS:

Choose among these four locations: the room you are now working in, your kitchen, your bedroom, or a workshop or garage you know well. In the circle below, identify your chosen location. Then write at least seven sensory details on this chart. Try to include at least one word or phrase for each sense.

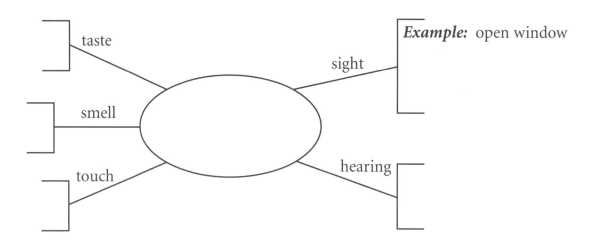

B. DIRECTIONS:

Review the *Writer's Manual,* pages 114 and 116 to 118, for advice on organizing details. Then select an order for organizing the details of your room description from Activity A. Divide the chart below into three to five columns, each column for providing details about one area (such as left, right, and straight ahead). At the top of each column, identify the area being described. Write at least three details in each column.

C. DIRECTIONS:

On a separate page or on a computer, write your description. Follow your outline above.

EXERCISE 25   Writing To Persuade

If you want others to share your opinion on an issue, try persuasive writing. To persuade others, you present your reasons, or arguments, in a logical order. Often, the most effective order is from least important to most important in order to leave readers with the best argument last. You can learn more about writing to persuade by reading page 115 of the *Writer's Manual*.

A. DIRECTIONS:

The arguments in the following persuasive paragraph are not arranged in an effective order. Underline the three arguments the writer gives for the new traffic light. Then rewrite just the arguments, this time arranging the reasons from least important to most important.

A new traffic light should be installed at the intersection of Main and Church Streets. Opponents may say that there are already too many traffic lights on Main, but I believe that the advantages of a signal outweigh the disadvantages. First, a traffic light may actually prevent a neighborhood child's death caused by a driver who speeds through the intersection without looking. A traffic light might also discourage people from using our congested street as a shortcut. Finally, a traffic light would give pedestrians a chance to cross the street safely. Please join the neighborhood group at City Hall tomorrow when we present our proposal for a new traffic light to the City Council.

_____

_____

_____

_____

_____

_____

B. DIRECTIONS:

Think of an issue about which you have definite opinions. It could be a question that faces your family, school, or community. Briefly describe the issue on the first line below. On the remaining lines, list at least three reasons for your views. Finally, number those reasons in order, from least to most important. See page 115 of the *Writer's Manual* for ideas for possible topics.

_____

_____

_____

_____

_____

_____

EXERCISE 26   Literary Terms and Devices

Writers often spice up their language by using special techniques, or devices. You will find a list of some of these techniques in the Literary Terms and Devices section of the *Writer's Manual* (pages 124–127). Use the definitions and examples you find there to complete the following exercise.

A. DIRECTIONS:

For each example, identify the literary technique that the writer has used. Underline the term that names that technique. If you need help, refer to pages 124 to 127 in the *Writer's Manual* for more information about each term and technique.

Example: You must be pulling my leg. (hyperbole, <u>idiom</u>)

1. The dull roar of highway traffic and the screech of brakes woke me up early the next morning. (rhyme, onomatopoeia)

2. When Carlo opened the window, a sweet, flowery fragrance filled the room. (simile, sensory detail)

3. We could barely see the candidate amid the snowstorm of confetti. (metaphor, personification)

4. I got my information straight from the horse's mouth. (idiom, sensory detail)

5. The day was so cold that when people talked, their words froze stiff in the air. (alliteration, hyperbole)

6. The mist-covered island called out invitingly to the sailor. (personification, simile)

7. *Humpty Dumpty sat on a wall.*
    Humpty Dumpty had a great fall. (rhyme, idiom)

8. He was as stubborn as a dog that won't give up its bone. (sensory detail, simile)

9. The new bike rider weaved, wobbled, and finally went down. (rhyme, alliteration)

10. I've felt as nervous as a cat all day. (cliché, metaphor)

B. DIRECTIONS:

Choose one of the literary devices listed below and circle it. On the lines, write a sentence using the device you chose.

alliteration	cliché	rhyme	sensory detail
hyperbole	idiom	metaphor	onomatopoeia
personification	simile		

ANSWER KEY

EXERCISE 1

A.

1. Spelling Checker, p. 9
   Spelling Rules, p. 67
   Spelling Using Phonics, p. 69
   Capitalization, p. 74
   Punctuation, p. 76
   Grammar, p. 84
2. pages 97–103 (or 104)
3. Any four of these: paragraph, friendly letter, business letter, story, daily journal, instructions, news article, description (writing to describe), persuasive composition (writing to persuade)

B.

2. Punctuation
3. Capitalization
4. Spelling Rules *or* Spelling Checker
5. Spelling Using Phonics *or* Spelling Checker
6. Spelling Checker
7. Grammar

EXERCISE 2

A.

1. bright, play, rent, whale
2. exist, handle, lever, profit
3. factory, family, fifty, flute
4. liberal, line, listen, little
5. example, excite, exhaust, expand
6. believe, bell, belong, belt

B.

1. li, 35
2. co, 18
3. or, 41
4. ba, 12
5. su, 57

EXERCISE 3

A.

1. symbol
2. dessert
3. flair
4. gait
5. dual
6. feint
7. hoarse
8. lessen

B.

Sentences will vary; each must include a homophone of the word listed below and use the homophone correctly.

1. aye
2. you
3. borough
4. due

EXERCISE 4

A.

1. foods
2. bodies
3. brushes
4. playing
5. videos
6. sheep
7. t's
8. pups
9. making
10. mice
11. nobly
12. baited

B.

1. prettier — e
2. finer — a
3. admitted — i (and/or k)
4. payment — f
5. gardener — l
6. notably — d
7. commitment — j (and/or k)
8. careful — b

C.

Sentences will vary. Each must include one of the words from Activity B, used and spelled correctly.

EXERCISE 5

A.

1. *Underline:* nieghbors; *Write:* neighbors
2. *Underline:* decieving; *Write:* deceiving
3. *Underline:* ilegal; *Write:* illegal
4. *Underline:* No-body; *Write:* Nobody
5. *Underline:* house-work;
   Write: housework

B.

1. rearranged
2. impossible
3. untouched
4. replaced
5. unjust

C.

Sentences will vary. Each must include one of the following possible compound words: blackout, boardwalk, outboard, outside, sideboard, sidewalk, walkout.

EXERCISE 6

1. *Underline:* told; *Write:* tolled
2. Correct
3. *Underline:* campanes; *Write:* campaigns
4. *Underline:* bolder; *Write:* boulder
5. *Underline:* seen; *Write:* scene
6. *Underline:* shabbie; *Write:* shabby
7. Correct
8. *Underline:* liberry; *Write:* library
9. *Underline:* innosent; *Write:* innocent
10. *Underline:* Counsel; *Write:* Council
11. *Underline:* fairy; *Write:* ferry
12. Correct
13. *Underline:* kemicals; *Write:* chemicals
14. *Underline:* locayshun; *Write:* location
15. Correct
16. *Underline:* overbored; *Write:* overboard
17. *Underline:* stationery; *Write:* stationary
18. *Underline:* graff; *Write:* graph
19. *Underline:* hamer; *Write:* hammer
20. *Underline:* definition; *Write:* definition

EXERCISE 7

A.

1. Brenda is head cashier at the Bigger Burger just east of town.
2. Last Friday, the Irish ambassador arrived in the United States.
3. Everyone knows that Labor Day marks the end of summer.
4. My ethnic background is a mixture of Mexican, German, and French.
5. Ivan plans to begin classes at the University of Arizona next September.
6. I attend the United Congregational Church on Delancey Street.

B.

Sentences will vary but must include an example of the category specified at the left.

EXERCISE 8

A.

1. The, Fasten
2. *Macavity* (each time it appears), *He's, His, And*
3. The
4. Tell
5. Our, Stephen, Crane, The, Red, Badge, Courage
6. (first word in each line) *Water, And, Water, Nor*

B.

Answers will vary. The title should be capitalized correctly. Underlining and quotation marks are not required.

EXERCISE 9

A.

1. Correct
2. !
3. .
4. Correct
5. ?
6. Correct

B.

Dear Marisa,

How are you? I can't believe that I haven't seen you since your birthday on April 25, 1995. So much has happened since then. Cheryl, my best friend, has moved to Albany, New York. After she left, I felt lonely for a while. But I have taken up some hobbies. Now I run, swim, and play tennis. Some friends recently asked, "Why not play handball?" I guess that will be my next sport.

I have also done some traveling. I discovered that I like the warm, friendly, slow-paced atmosphere of the South. I just heard about a sports convention that will be held in Atlanta, Georgia, and I am planning to attend. I read that over 10,000 people attended the organization's last convention.

I hope to see you soon. Maybe I can stop by on my way to Atlanta on September 6, 1997.

Your cousin,

Leslie

EXERCISE 10

A.

1. "I'm sure you would enjoy a visit to Australia," said the travel agent.
2. Lee asked, "Which instrument do you play in the orchestra?"

3. "I can't figure out how to program this answering machine," complained Dardreana.
4. The eye doctor asked, "Can you read the first line of letters on the chart?"
5. "The marchers will start at Public Square and go all the way to the lakefront," explained the news announcer.
6. Steve shouted, "I got tickets to the play-off game!"
7. "Be careful when you pick up that glass figurine," warned Marquita.
8. The worried astronaut said, "Houston, we have a problem."
9. "I believe that my experience qualifies me for this job," asserted James.
10. "The loss of our rain forests is a global problem," reported the scientist.

B.
Quotations will vary. All quotations should be punctuated correctly.

Exercise 11

A.
1. farmer's
2. skaters'
3. chairman's
4. Watson and Crick's
5. grandmother's
6. Dr. Simmons's
7. someone else's
8. Muellers'
9. Carmen and Gina's
10. editor-in-chief's

B.
1. couldn't
2. she'll
3. we'd
4. I'm
5. won't
6. I've
7. can't
8. he's
9. we're
10. what's

Exercise 12

A.
Answers will vary but must result in complete sentences. Sample answers are given.
1. **Many drivers** bought lottery tickets at the gas station.
2. **My old watch** has a habit of being slow.
3. **Your nightmares** may return late at night.
4. **A flock of geese** flew north over the lake.

B.
Answers will vary but must result in complete sentences. Sample answers are given.
1. Every salesperson in the store **was busy with a customer.**
2. The twins **rarely dress alike.**
3. My two closest friends **went out of town this weekend.**
4. Many flowers in the garden **bloom during the spring.**

C.
1. sentence
2. subject
3. phrase
4. predicate
5. predicate

Exercise 13

A.
1. knows
2. exit
3. enjoy
4. cites
5. bloom
6. select

B.
1. are
2. are
3. is
4. am
5. are
6. are

C.
Sentences will vary, but must use one of the specified verb forms. Be sure that the verb agrees with the subject in both number and person.

Exercise 14

A.
1. are digging
2. will take
3. has filled
4. will be
5. are blocking
6. will pop
7. have formed
8. played
9. will tackle
10. have waited
11. wilted
12. has been

B.
1. has swum
2. has caught
3. have taken
4. have worn
5. have been

Exercise 15

1. *Underline:* at the Corner Cafe; *Write:* meal
2. *Circle:* tasteless; *Write:* salad
3. *Underline:* remarkably; *Write:* adjective
4. *Write:* in, of, at
5. *Underline:* of cold mashed potatoes; *Circle:* cold, mashed; *Box:* potatoes
6. (a) *Underline:* there, obviously, rather, loudly
   (b) *Write H above:* obviously, loudly; *Write W above:* there; *Write T above:* rather
   (c) *Write:* 5
7. Answers will vary but must include the listed elements. *Sample answer:* **Unhappy customers won't return to that restaurant soon.**

Exercise 16

A.
1. The mountain climbers set out although snow was beginning to fall.
2. During the storm, a tree fell on a car that belonged to Darlene Stewart.
3. Keith waved to Rosa at the mall yesterday, but she didn't notice him.
4. I am the talented dancer whom you are looking for. *Or:* I am the talented dancer for whom you are looking.
5. We threw out the old blue vase, which was leaking.
6. The storm may stay out at sea, or it may clobber the coast.

B.
Answers will vary but must consist of correct sentences. *Possible answer:*
Baby Janice loves to listen to stories. She always behaves for sitters who know many stories and tell them well.

Exercise 17

A.
Answers will vary. If asked, student should be able to state the link between the chosen topic and his or her answers.

B.
Answers will vary. If asked, student should be able to describe the relationship between the selected topic and each detail listed.

Exercise 18

Explanations may vary, but detailed steps must be arranged in chronological order as indicated by the numbering in the notes.

Exercise 19

Wording of answers 1–4 will vary, but the answers must include the following concepts:
1. The revision avoided the repetition of the word *map*. *Optional:* In addition, the verb *find* gives a more active tone to the passage.
2. The original last sentence was off the topic, place names in Ohio.
3. The sentence about Athens, Antioch, and Alexandria fits better with the listing of names from different countries than with the sentences about pronunciation of names.
4. The original sentence was too long; the material is easier to understand when the second idea is presented in a separate sentence.
5. *Preferred answer:* The paragraph needs an ending sentence because the material should be pulled together and given a focus. However, accept the alternative if a logical and relevant reason is provided.

Exercise 20

1. *Marks:* a caret (pointing either up or down) and an apostrophe between *n* and *t* of *wont*; a period marked after *Dr*; three short lines under *c* of *campbell*; a circle around the 6 and *sp* written above the numeral; a slant line through the *M* of *Months*
   Correction: You won't need to see Dr. Campbell until six months from now.
2. *Marks:* a slant line through *P* of *Program*; a deletion line through the comma; a line through the word *has*, possibly with a caret pointing up to the correction; a caret pointing up between the *h* and *s* of *glitchs*
   Correction: The latest versions of that computer program have several glitches.

3. *Marks:* curved lines connecting the *p* and the *s* of *up-stairs* and, possibly, a deletion sign through the hyphen of that word; deletion signs through both sets of quotation marks; a line through *too*, possibly with a caret pointing up to the correction
   Correction: My neighbor upstairs said that she was going to retire soon.
4. *Marks:* a caret over a comma following *car;* three short lines under the *i;* a caret over a comma following *it;* and three short lines under the *j* of *jack*
   Correction: Mailee steered the car, I pushed it, and Jack just stood and watched.
5. *Marks:* a caret and an apostrophe between the *t* and *s* of *Its;* a period after *Ms;* a paragraph sign between the two sentences; a caret and an apostrophe between the *I* and *m* of *Im;* and three short lines under the *j* of *junior*
   Correction: "It's time for bed," Ms. Kantor said.
   "I'm not tired," Junior objected.
6. *Marks:* a line through *beautyful* and, possibly, a caret pointing to the correction; a slant line through the *s* in *sky;* and a caret between *full* and *stars,* possibly pointing to the addition *of*
   Correction: How beautiful the sky is tonight, full of stars!
7. *Marks:* a deletion line through the apostrophe after *Smith's* and curved lines connecting the *h* of *Smith's* and the following *s;* three short lines under the *a* of *africa;* and a line through *they're,* possibly with a caret pointing to the correction
   Correction: The Smiths went to Africa on their vacation.
8. *Marks:* curved lines connecting the words *bed* and *room;* a line through *payed* and, possibly, a caret pointing to the correction; and a question mark after *yet*
   Correction: Has the furniture in the bedroom been paid for yet?

EXERCISE 21

A.

1. c.
2. d.
3. b.
4. a.
5. e.

B.

3579 Wood Road
Los Angeles, CA 90048
October 31, 1997

Dear Aunt Lucy,
   (Indent first line. Letters will vary, but should express gratitude for a gift.)
(Closings will vary.)   Your nephew,
                  Dave

EXERCISE 22

A.
Characters, settings, and conflicts will vary. There should be a clear differentiation between those connected with personal experiences and those connected with fantasies.

B.
All elements of the plot will vary. Be sure that events follow logically and in time order.

C.
Be sure that the story has a title and an introduction. Plot events should be arranged in time order. The story should include details and descriptions not explicitly mentioned in the story map planned above.

EXERCISE 23

A.
Instructions should begin with a topic sentence and end with a conclusion, both of which will vary. Topic sentence example: ***Baking bread is an age-old art, one that takes time and patience.*** Conclusion example: ***Now it's time to eat the best bread you have ever tasted.*** The steps should be arranged in the following order:

• First, stir together all the ingredients, beating until the mixture is smooth.
• Take the smooth mixture and knead it on a floured board for about ten minutes.
• After you finish kneading the dough, place it in a greased bowl and wait about an hour for it to rise the first time.
• Punch down the risen dough, roll it into a rectangle, roll it up, and put it in a pan.
• Let the dough rise again in the pan.
• Last, bake the bread at 425 degrees for about 35 minutes.

B.
The steps listed should be clearly related to the task chosen. The steps should be numbered in the order in which they are to be completed. In the second part of the activity, the complete written instructions should begin with an introductory topic sentence that states the task that will be explained. The steps should follow time order as specified in the list.

EXERCISE 24

A.
Answers will vary but should include details referring to at least three of the senses.

B.
Answers will vary. There must be at least two columns/groups of details, preferably three or four.

C.
Descriptions will vary. Check for correspondence to listed details, and for clarity of organization and ease of following the spatial order.

EXERCISE 25

A.
The following sentences should be underlined:
First, a traffic light may actually prevent a neighborhood child's death caused by a driver who speeds through the intersection without looking. A traffic light might also discourage people from using our congested street as a shortcut. Finally, a traffic light would give pedestrians a chance to cross the street safely.
   The wording of the rewritten arguments may vary slightly, but the order should be as follows:

• A traffic light might discourage people from using our congested street as a shortcut.
• A traffic light would give pedestrians a chance to cross the street safely.
• A traffic light may actually prevent a neighborhood child's death caused by a driver who speeds through the intersection without looking.

B.
Issues and reasons will vary. Reasons should be numbered from least to most important.

EXERCISE 26

A.

1. onomatopoeia
2. sensory detail
3. metaphor
4. idiom
5. hyperbole
6. personification
7. rhyme
8. simile
9. alliteration
10. cliché

B.
Sentences will vary. Be sure the sentence uses the technique that was circled.

WRITER'S MANUAL ACTIVITY BOOK 2

Student Activity Skillbooks

	Order Number
Phonics and Whole Words Activity Book 1	0887-3*
Phonics and Whole Words Activity Book 2	0888-1*
Introductory Word Book Activity Book	0890-3*
Writer's Manual Activity Book 1	0891-1*
Writer's Manual Activity Book 2	0893-8*

Reading and Writing Handbooks

	Order Number
1000 Instant Words	0880-6
Phonics Patterns	0879-2
Introductory Word Book	0877-6
Writer's Manual	0878-4

*Available only in packages of 10. To order, use number listed above.

CONTEMPORARY BOOKS

a division of NTC/CONTEMPORARY PUBLISHING GROUP

ISBN: 0-8092-0893-8

90000

9 780809 208937

ISBN 0-8092-0893-8